APATOSAURUS

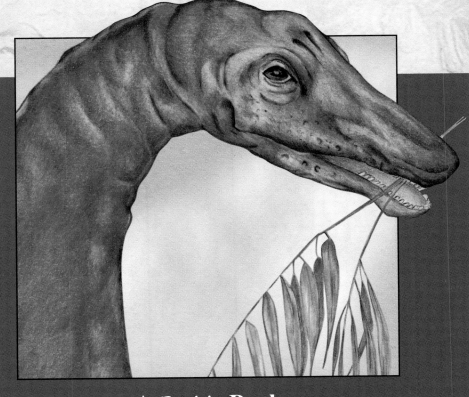

A Buddy Book
by
Richard M. Gaines

ABDO
Publishing Company

VISIT US AT

www.abdopub.com

Published by ABDO Publishing Company, 4940 Viking Drive, Edina, Minnesota 55435. Copyright © 2001 by Abdo Consulting Group, Inc. International copyrights reserved in all countries. No part of this book may be reproduced in any form without written permission from the publisher.

Printed in the United States.

Edited by: Christy DeVillier
Contributing editors: Mike Goecke, Matt Ray
Graphic Design: Denise Esner, Maria Hosley
Cover Art: Denise Esner, title page
Interior Photos/Illustrations: page 4: Joe Tucciarone; pages 6, 7, 14 & 17: M. Shiraish ©1999 All Rights Reserved; page 9: Denise Esner; page 13: ©Douglas Henderson from *Riddle of the Dinosaur* by John Noble Wilford, published by Knopf; page 15: Maria Hosley; page 21: ©Douglas Henderson; page 23: Jodi Henderson; page 27: Corbis.

Library of Congress Cataloging-in-Publication Data

Gaines, Richard, 1942-
    Apatosaurus/Richard M. Gaines.
      p. cm. – (Dinosaurs)
    Includes index.
    ISBN 1-57765-487-0
    1. Apatosaurus—Juvenile literature. [1. Apatosaurus. 2. Dinosaurs.] I. Title.

QE862.S3 G34 2001
567.913'8—dc21

00-048532

TABLE OF CONTENTS

WHAT WERE THEY?

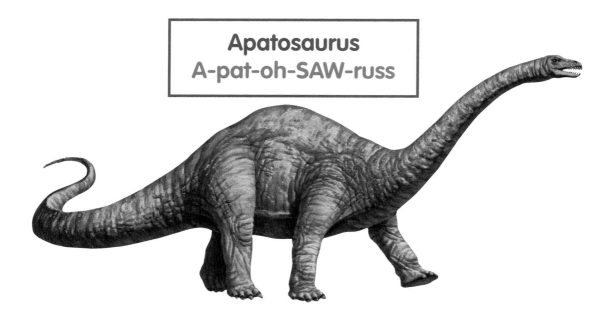

Apatosaurus
A-pat-oh-SAW-russ

The Apatosaurus was one of the largest animals ever. People used to call this giant dinosaur a Brontosaurus. It lived 150 million years ago during the late Jurassic period.

4

The Apatosaurus's nickname is "Long Neck." Can you guess why? Its neck was 40 feet (12 m) long. "Long Neck's" tail was 40 feet (12 m) long, too.

"Long Neck" grew to be 90 feet (27 m) long. It stood 15 feet (5 m) tall at the hips. It weighed up to 70,000 pounds (31,751 kg). About five elephants weigh that much!

Paleontologists study fossils of the Apatosaurus's footprints. We call these footprint fossils trackways. These paleontologists learned that the Apatosaurus walked on all four legs. The back legs were larger and longer than its front legs.

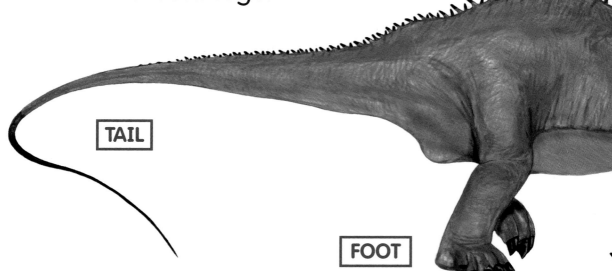

TAIL

FOOT

In one day, the Apatosaurus walked about 10 miles (16 km). It carried its tail straight out as it moved. Why? This whip-like tail helped to balance the huge Apatosaurus.

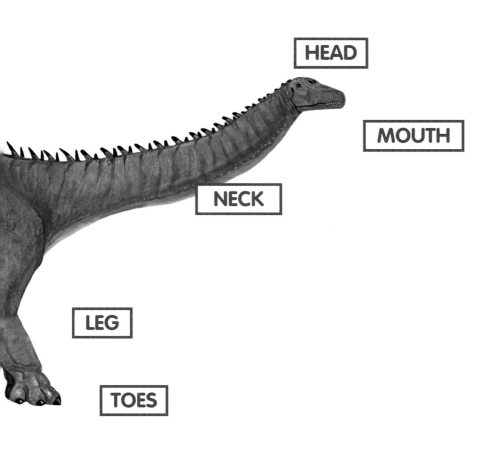

HEAD

MOUTH

NECK

LEG

TOES

WHY WAS IT SPECIAL?

The Apatosaurus's long neck was very important. This giant could stretch its long neck into the forest to eat. The Apatosaurus's long neck helped it reach special plants and leaves.

The Apatosaurus's neck was strong. It was made up of light, strong bones. This neck also had a long ligament. A ligament is like a thick rubber band. The Apatosaurus easily held its head up with such a strong neck.

WHERE DID THEY LIVE?

Apatosaurus lived in western North America. In the late Jurassic period, this continent was 400 miles (644 km) south of where it is today.

The climate was warmer and drier 150 million years ago. Most of the time, it did not rain. Yet, there were a few rainy periods throughout the year.

During these rainy periods, the rainwater formed rivers and streams. These rivers and streams flowed eastward to the flat lands, or prairies.

Prairie

WHAT WAS THE LAND LIKE?

Paleontologists used to believe the Apatosaurus lived near water. Now, they think the Apatosaurus spent most of its time on land.

What kinds of trees grew where the Apatosaurus lived? There were several kinds of evergreen, or conifer, trees. Ginkgoes and cycads were there, too.

There were many kinds of ferns growing where the Apatosaurus lived. One kind of fern tree grew 70 feet (21 m) tall. Other ferns were more like bushes. Another kind of fern only grew along the ground.

Sauropods walking through the cycad and ginkgo trees.

The Apatosaurus lived among other dinosaurs. Two of these are the Brachiosaurus and the Dryosaurus.

The Brachiosaurus weighed over 100,000 pounds (45,359 kg). It held its neck up in the air like a giraffe. It could reach trees almost 100 feet (30 m) away.

Brachiosaurus

The Dryosaurus weighed about 150 pounds (68 kg). It was 10 feet (3 m) long. This dinosaur walked around on two legs. Herds of them ran over the wide prairies eating ferns.

The Dryosaurus had special teeth that stayed sharp. This dinosaur could store food in its cheeks.

Dryosaurus

WHO ELSE LIVED THERE?

Which other interesting animals lived among the Apatosaurus? Turtles, crocodiles, and lizards lived near water. They favored lakes, rivers, and streams. Small mammals lived in the woods.

One mammal, the Ornitholestes, was larger than the biggest dog. It had long arms and clawed fingers. Sharp teeth filled its long mouth.

Ornitholestes

Some of the insects that lived 150 million years ago are still around today. Some of these insects are ants, wasps, cockroaches, dragonflies, and termites. Giant communities of termites ate the rotting wood of the forests. Back then, some termite mounds were over 100 feet (30 m) high.

WHAT DID THEY EAT?

The Apatosaurus was an herbivore, or plant-eater. It ate ferns, ginkgoes, conifers, and cycads. It could eat 500 pounds (226 kg) of food each day.

How did the the Apatosaurus eat? This plant-eater had teeth in the front of its mouth. These teeth were dull and pencil-shaped. It used these teeth to peel the leaves from plants and trees. The Apatosaurus did not use its teeth to chew. Instead, this great dinosaur swallowed the food whole.

The Apatosaurus swallowed rocks from the ground. We call these rocks gastroliths or gizzard stones. These rocks helped to break down the food in the Apatosaurus's stomach.

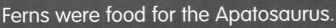
Ferns were food for the Apatosaurus.

The big meat-eating dinosaurs, or carnivores, were the Apatosaurus's enemies. The giant Apatosaurus had to watch out for these enemies.

One enemy of the Apatosaurus was the Allosaurus. The Allosaurus was two feet (61 cm) shorter than the Apatosaurus. So, the Apatosaurus could fight the shorter dinosaur and win. The Apatosaurus could fight with its big, clawed front feet.

A meat-eater on the hunt.

The Apatosaurus could not fight a pack of Allosaurus, though. A group of 40 Allosaurus could eat an entire 40,000-pound (18,144-kg) Apatosaurus in just one day.

FAMILY LIFE

The Apatosaurus belongs to a family of dinosaurs called Sauropods. Sauropod dinosaurs laid their eggs in pairs in a straight line. Sauropod eggs are shaped like footballs.

Apatosaurus babies were about five feet (two m) long. It took over 20 years for these babies to grow up into adults. The Apatosaurus could live over 100 years.

Eggs

The Apatosaurus likely traveled in family-sized groups. Young Apatosaurus walked in the middle of the herd. The adults stayed on the outside of the group. These adults were guarding the young dinosaurs from enemies.

THE FAMILY TREE

The Sauropods lived in North America. All Sauropods have long necks. Two Sauropod dinosaurs, the Barosaurus and the Diplodocus, were bigger than the Apatosaurus. The Seismosaurus and the Supersaurus were even bigger.

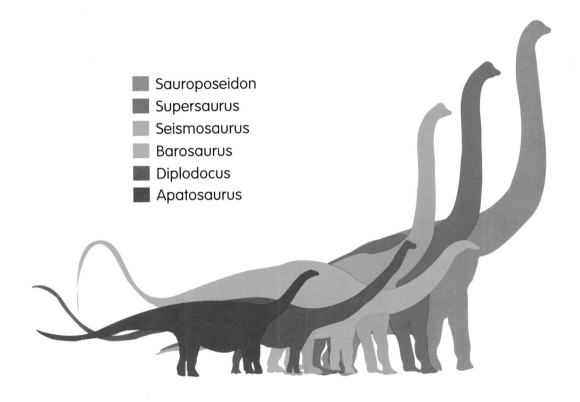

Sauroposeidon
Supersaurus
Seismosaurus
Barosaurus
Diplodocus
Apatosaurus

Paleontologists believe the Sauroposeidon was the biggest land animal ever. This giant Sauropod was taller than a five-story building.

DISCOVERY

In 1877, someone discovered a dinosaur fossil in Colorado. They found most of the dinosaur's bones. But they could not find the head.

At first, everyone thought this fossil was from a Camarasaurus dinosaur. Later, they found out this was a mistake.

Who discovered the mistake? It was Othniel C. Marsh. He is a famous fossil hunter. He said this dinosaur fossil was not from a Camarasaurus. It really belonged to the Apatosaurus.

Apatosaurus fossil

WHERE ARE THEY TODAY?

American Museum of Natural History
Central Park West at 79th Street
New York, NY 10024
www.amnh.org

The Carnegie Museum in Pittsburgh
4400 Forbes Avenue
Pittsburgh, PA 15213
www.carnegiemuseums.org/cmnh

The Museum of Western Colorado
462 Ute Avenue
Grand Junction, CO 81501
Mailing Address: P.O. Box 20000,
Grand Junction, CO 81502-5020
www.wcmuseum.org

APATOSAURUS

NAME MEANS	Tricky Lizard
DIET	Plants
WEIGHT	70,000 pounds (31,751 kg)
HEIGHT	70 feet (21 m)
TIME	Late Jurassic Period
FAMILY	Sauropod
SPECIAL FEATURE	Long neck
FOSSILS FOUND	USA—Colorado, Oklahoma, Utah, Wyoming

Apatosaurus lived
150 million years ago.

First humans appeared
1.6 million years ago.

Triassic Period	Jurassic Period	Cretaceous Period	Tertiary Period
245 Million years ago	208 Million years ago	144 Million years ago	65 Million years ago

Mesozoic Era | Cenozoic Era

FUN DINOSAUR WEB SITES

Zoom Dinosaurs
www.EnchantedLearning.com/subjects/dinosaurs
Zoom Dinosaurs, designed for students of all ages,
includes an illustrated dinosaur dictionary and classroom
activities.

Fossil Zone: The Place to Dig
www.discovery.com/exp/fossilzone/fossilzone.html
Hear dinosaur sounds, see dinosaurs in motion, find
dinosaur fossils, and build a dinosaur at this site.

Dinosaur/Extinction
www.cotf.edu/ete/modules/msese/dinosaur.html
This series of web pages explains possible theories of why
dinosaurs died out.

carnivore a meat-eater.

climate the weather (rain, temperature, and wind) of a place.

conifer trees that have needles instead of leaves. Conifers stay green all year long.

continent one of the seven large land masses on earth.

cycads palmlike plants or trees.

dinosaur reptiles that lived on land 248–65 million years ago.

fossil remains of very old animals and plants. People commonly find fossils in the ground.

gastroliths rocks the Apatosaurus ate, or gizzard stones.

ginkgoes trees with fan-shaped leaves and yellow seeds.

herbivore a plant-eater.

Jurassic period period of time that happened 208–146 million years ago.

mammals warm-blooded animals that feed milk to their young.

paleontologist someone who studies very old life (like dinosaurs), mostly by studying fossils.

prairie flat and grassy land.

Sauropod "Long Neck" family of dinosaurs. The Apatosaurus is a member of the Sauropod family.

trackways fossils of dinosaur footprints.

INDEX